C000260686

# MINI
## & MINI COOPER
### Colour Family Album

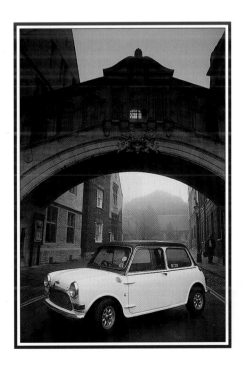

## DEDICATION
To Jenny Irving, the first truly whacky model we met, who has been a treasured
friend ever since.

First published in 1997 by Veloce Publishing Plc., 33, Trinity Street, Dorchester DT1 1TT, England. Fax: 01305 268864.

ISBN: 1 87 4105 79 0/UPC: 36847 00079 0

© 1997 Andrea & David Sparrow and Veloce Publishing Plc
All rights reserved. With the exception of quoting brief passages for the purpose of review, no part of this publication may be recorded, reproduced or
transmitted by any means, including photocopying, without the written permission of Veloce Publishing Plc.
Throughout this book logos, model names and designations, etc., may have been used for the purposes of identification, illustration and decoration. Such
names are the property of the trademark holder as this is not an official publication.
Readers with ideas for automotive books, or books on other transport or related hobby subjects, are invited to write to Veloce Publishing at the above address.

British Library Cataloguing in Publication Data -
A catalogue record for this book is available from the British Library.

Typesetting (Avant Garde), design and page make-up all by Veloce on AppleMac.
Printed in Hong Kong.

# ANDREA & DAVID SPARROW

**VELOCE PUBLISHING PLC**
PUBLISHERS OF FINE AUTOMOTIVE BOOKS

# THANKS

Roger Wall, Henk and Roel Cremers, Rob Fetlaar, Brigitte, Lilian, Nico and Theo Geraedts, Anton Saris, Mike Scarfe, Brian Preston, Sue Creed, Scott Lloyd, Andy Saunders, Emma Kirke, Clive Powell, Geoff Tuley of Yorkshire Car Collection, Stephen Smith, Jeremy Ross, Tracy Napier, Gemma Triance, Sue Birch, Tony Miles, Lance and Tracy Peacock, Pauline Chart, Sian Hellyar, Mike Brown, Edward Armstrong, Ken Bateman, John Parnell, Michael Mark, Armin Waldkoetter, Lindsay Haynes, Ingrid, Roger, Jenny and Debbie Knott, Graham Robinson,

Joanna Yoffey of David Clarke Associates, *Mini World Magazine*, John Brigden of British Motor Heritage, Sally Fitzgerald and Jane Rowell of A's of Herts, SALT Organisation, Fraser Davies of Mini-Moto, Mini Seven Club Netherlands, Trevor Morgan and Don Shaw of Capespan, Peter and Phil Hines, Graham Phillips, John Aulman and Karen Porter at Somerford Mini, Jane Carney of Himley Hall, John Hopson of Summit Garage, Castle Coombe Circuit. Julie Richards and Andy Rushton of the National Hockey Centre.

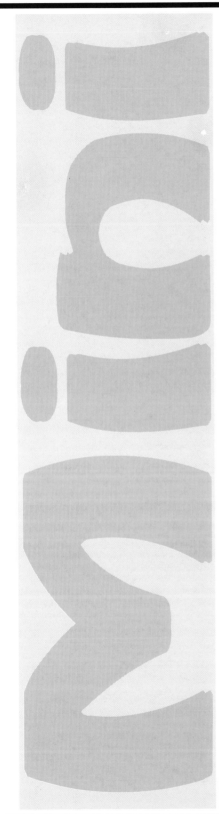

# CONTENTS

# INTRODUCTION

Surely anyone in Britain who remembers the sixties will have fond memories of the Mini. At some point in the sixties or seventies, you either owned one, learned to drive in one, dated someone with one, or sadly could not afford one. If you were to be transported back to those heady days, of course, you would discover that the ride was not so very comfortable, and that older models came with free 'indoor rain'; that wasn't the point. In the sixties the Mini was not just a car, but part of a whole new way of life. Post-war austerities had given way to new freedoms - of movement, of expression, and of views. This was the car being seen increasingly on the streets, the car that was winning the Monte Carlo Rally, the car that everyone wanted. The production life of the Mini has spanned three distinct eras - BMC, Leyland and Rover. And woven into the first and last of these eras is the amazing Cooper success story. Clearly the Mini has earned the accolade of a true classic.

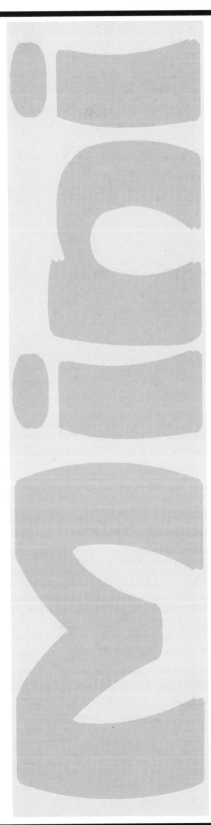

# A SMALL CAR IS NEEDED

## 1

The concept of a small, frugal car, priced within the reach of ordinary working folk with families to support was certainly not new. In the first five post-war years, two 'cars for the people' appeared which had been under development before the war: the Citroen 2CV took off in France and the Volkswagen Beetle was introduced in Germany. Messerschmitt, Isetta and Heinkel, meanwhile, along

*BMC Head Leonard Lord realised there was an opening in the market for a small car. (Mini Special: 1979).*

*Overleaf: A well-travelled Mini. This 1098cc Clubman, a 'Margrave', styled by the Wood & Pickett company of Pimlico, London, took part in the 1991 Paris to Moscow run, coming home a highly respectable 16th overall.*

*'Little Miss Pink Knickers' attracts attention wherever she goes, warming even the coldest of hearts. Sue Creed's Mini started life as a Piccadilly, but now has a 1300 MG Metro engine - fitted by Sue. The bonnet is a specially made steel panel. (Originally Mini Piccadilly: 1986).*

with many other less-famous manufacturers, pushed at the limits of size with their microcars.

A less-recognised concern was Duncan Industries of Norfolk. Their main activity was the design and assembly of body shells and interiors to fit the chassis of manufacturers such as Alvis and Healey. But during 1947 their engineer, Alan Lamburn, was hard at work designing a small car. His brief was to provide 'arm-chairs for two and accommo-dation for three'. A prototype was ready for testing by the autumn of 1948.

*Edward Armstrong's meticulously restored Police Mini spent its working life in the Birmingham area - catching many criminals in supposedly sportier vehicles who doubtless underestimated the Mini's abilities. (Austin Mini Cooper S: 1968).*

The little car was named 'Dragonfly', and was remarkable for its transversely mounted engine, front-wheel drive, small wheels and rubber suspension. Unfortunately, things were not going well for Duncan Industries. An increase in purchase tax on more expensive cars caused a slump in the market, and the company was soon in dire straights and looking for a buyer for its assets, which included the little Dragonfly. BSA, and then Jaguar, turned down the opportunity, but their plight came to the attention of Austin managing director Leonard Lord, who recognised potential when he saw it.

Lord had been toying with the idea of adding a small car to his range for some time. However, he had no intention of putting the Dragonfly itself into production: it was pretty in a curvaceous, slightly Italian way, and delivered spectacular performance thanks to its lightness and innovative design, but it was not perfect. Lord hoped that his staff at Longbridge would be inspired by the little car to produce something that would be a world-beater. The man in charge of the mission would

Minis line up at the start of the London Lord Mayor's Show procession in November 1996. More than thirty cars were given a rapturous reception during the drive. The television cameras lingered on the Minis until they were right out of sight!

Roger Wall's exotic Mini was originally owned by King Constantine of Greece. Later it was sold to actor Lawrence Harvey, who had Wood and Pickett create this elegant effect with no side windows but with pram irons and an oval rear window. (Wood & Pickett Margrave-style Mini: 1965).

*Inset: There have been several experimental Mini research projects that have only recently seen the light of day. This one was for engine development, although the car has an odd-shaped front. (experimental Mini: 1978).*

be Alec Issigonis.

Alexander Issigonis was born in Smyrna (now in Turkey but then part of Greece) in 1906. His mother was German, his father a naturalised British citizen of Greek descent. After his father's death, fifteen-year-old Alec and his mother settled in London, where he attended college before launching himself on his chosen career in engineering.

At the age of thirty Issigonis joined Morris as part of the team working on new suspension systems, and it was here that he met Leonard Lord.

Issigonis was responsible for designing the Morris Minor; then he left what was by then BMC for four years, returning to the fold in 1956 to start work on a new mid-range family car. But the Suez oil crisis intervened; normal size family saloons, however brilliant, had suddenly lost their appeal. Leonard Lord realised that now was the time for the small car to become reality and in March 1957 Issigonis was

*The Mini found its niche in the swinging sixties, although this Mini's concealed door hinges indicate it was made during a later decade. (Mini: 1979).*

*The Mini is a very British institution ... (Morris Mini MkII: 1969).*

*Commercial Minis - vans and pick-ups - often piled on the miles. But this lovely blue van stayed with its first owner for twenty-eight years, clocking up just 23,800 miles! (Morris Minivan: 1968).*

was a man of extraordinary vision and considerable stubbornness - his team well knew when it was worth arguing a point, and when it was not. His major preoccupation was the car's size: it had to be small. He concluded that front-wheel drive was essential. The development of a completely new engine would have been the ideal solution, but that was an impossible expense for the company, and Issigonis realised that he would have to adapt the A-series engine already in use in the Morris Minor.

His solution was both elegant and innovative. In addition to mounting the engine transversely, he sited the gearbox underneath it, so that the two used the same oil supply. This flash of genius solved at a single stroke one of the biggest problems - keeping the car's overall dimensions small. Prototypes were soon up and running. Experiments with an increase in engine capacity eventually gave rise to a unit of 848cc, which gave 34bhp and propelled the little car to an adequate and quite respectable 74mph.

There were initial problems with bodywork. Attaching the engine directly to the body-

instructed to get his team together and go to work on the project, which was code-named ADO15.

Issigonis was in charge, and there were certain aspects of the project that would be non-negotiable. He

Left: These boots are made
for driving. (Austin Seven
De Luxe: 1962).

Of course, not all Mini Pick-ups have led sedate working lives ... (Mini Pick-up: 1980).

work caused unacceptable stress to the metalwork. The solution was to build the car around subframes: the front one bearing the engine plus gearbox unit, steering and front suspension; the rear supporting the rear suspension.

Intrusion into the valuable interior space was minimised by using tiny ten-inch wheels, and the harshness of ride which this caused was offset by an ingenious rubber cone suspension system. Elsewhere simplicity was all: fussy styling, complex panel shapes and expensive extras were just not the Issigonis way. Knowing that he would not personally be tempted by extravagant style, he firmly believed that no-one else would either. He was equally dismissive of marketing concepts, convinced that a good product was all that counted. More to the point, he knew that cost was the most important factor for most buyers, and that a good product at the right price would sell.

Leonard Lord drove his first Mini - in prototype form - in the summer of 1958, and he was impressed. He instructed the team to have the car in production within the year - a tall order. In truth, the Mini could have done with another six months, or so, of pre-launch development before it hit the streets, but there was much in its favour to outweigh the problems. A few pre-production examples were built by Austin at Longbridge and Morris at Cowley before production began in earnest. The Austin Seven and Morris Mini Minor were made available for the press to drive at a special presentation on 18 August 1959, and were rapturously received. The *Birmingham Evening Mail,* ecstatic about the car's get-up-and-go, 74mph top speed and ease of parking, enthused: 'On the face of it, BMC have produced something that is new, exciting and practical - a cheap-to-run car that will accommodate a small family, hold its own in a main-road traffic stream, and park on a postage stamp.' The Mini was delivering just what had been asked of it!

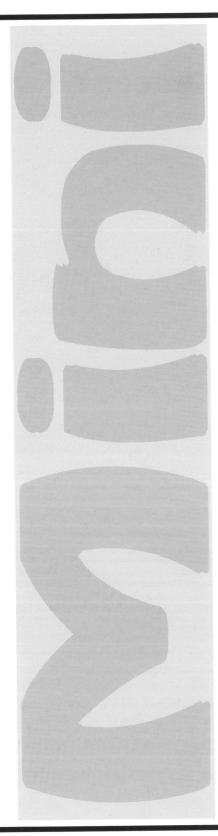

# THE MINI EVOLVES

Launches of new cars had traditionally been rather staid and stuffy affairs. After all, buying a car was serious stuff: serious amounts of money were going to be spent by serious people, so the mood had to be, well, serious. Tony Ball had other ideas. As organiser of the Mini's debut, he decided to try something different, more along the lines of Harley Earl's Motorama shows in the USA. He would put on an extravaganza - an unusual and mould-breaking introduction to match the car.

The launch date had been planned initially for 2 September, but it was brought forward to 26th August.

Dressed in a magician's top hat and tails, Tony Ball introduced the new car, first to the press, then later to the assembled Morris and Austin dealers. Flamboyantly, he

*An automatic option was first announced in 1965, although production did not get underway until the following year. (Austin Mini 1000 Automatic: 1968).*

*Minis would become a sixties icon - in both car and skirt form.*
*(Austin Seven De Luxe: 1962).*

*Issigonis's brilliant feat of engineering - a transversely mounted engine with the gearbox underneath - was the major factor in keeping the car 'mini'. (Austin Seven: 1962 and Morris Mini Minor: 1960).*

ence on the young, which also helped its popularity - after a faltering start it was set on the road to success.

Although it would continue to be made in both Austin and Morris guises for ten years, everyone soon forgot separate names and images, and the word 'Mini' passed into general use.

Both the first Austin Seven and the first Morris Mini Minor came in two versions - the basic and the De Luxe (which for £40 more, provided extras such as windscreen washers, a higher level of trim with added chrome touches, more comfortable seats and opening rear windows). Fixing points for seat belts, which Issigonis had

stepped in. The Mini was a whizz in cities, where traffic was starting to be a real problem. It parked in a tiny little space, whipped in and out of traffic, and was inexpensive to run. It started to be trendy, a fashion accessory, a must-have. The Mini was denounced by establishment figures as a really bad influ-

failed to provide, were added late in 1960.

In June the following year the Super version was introduced, featuring two-tone paintwork and better interior appointment and trim. The Austin's face became a little more familiar later that same year with the introduction of the chrome front grille, while the Morris's Super version appeared with a distinctive ten horizontal bar grille. At the start of 1962 the Austin Seven model was rechristened the Austin Mini. (The name 'Austin Seven' had been chosen for reasons of nostalgia, but it had come to sound distinctly old-fashioned). Later that year both Austin and Morris De Luxe and Super models were superseded by Super De Luxe versions.

Hydrolastic suspension was introduced in 1964. The system had been developed by Issigonis in collaboration with Alex Moulton. It was supposed to eliminate the Mini's rather bumpy ride, but it tended to replace it with a pitch-and-toss effect which many drivers found equally unpleasant. As it was also a more expensive system, it is not surprising that it lasted only five years on the standard Mini. During 1966, production of the automatic began some considerable time after its announcement.

Of these first Minis, 435,500 Austin and 510,000 Morris units were built.

*The Austin Countryman and Morris Traveller echoed traditional estate style with wooden framing - on Minis the woodwork was purely cosmetic.*
*(Austin Mini Countryman: 1965).*

*The Mini vans, pick-ups and estate versions were built on a longer wheelbase version of the Mini's floorpan. (Morris Minivan: 1968).*

In October 1967 the MkII Mini arrived. The Morris version dropped the 'Minor' from its title, so the choice was now Austin Mini or Morris Mini. Both were available in three versions: the standard 850cc, or the Super De Luxe with either the 850cc or the 1000cc engine on which the Mini Cooper engines were based (actually a 998cc unit giving 38bhp and a maximum speed of 75mph). At the same time the shape of the grilles was changed slightly, and there was a larger rear window and bigger rear light clusters.

In 1968 the Cooper's fully synchromeshed four-speed gearbox was fitted. That year BMC merged with the Leyland company, and Mini production at Cowley ended, all production now taking place at Longbridge. By the end of 1969 the final Minis with Austin or Morris tags had rolled off the production line. Of these MkII Minis, 154,000 Austin and 206,000 Morris units were built.

As the sixties drew to a close, BMC was transformed into British Leyland, and the age of the MkIII Mini, the BL Mini, began. There was to be one basic 850 model, a 1000cc version, the newly introduced Clubman,

*The Clubman - beloved by some, but despised by many as a betrayal of the classic Mini shape.
(Mini Clubman: 1978).*

the 850cc or the 1000cc engine on which the Mini Cooper engines were based (actually a 998cc unit giving 38bhp and a maximum speed of 75mph). At the same time the shape of the grilles was changed slightly, and there was a larger rear window and bigger rear light clusters.

In 1968 the Cooper's fully synchromeshed four-speed gearbox was fitted. That year BMC merged with the Leyland company, and Mini production at Cowley ended, all production now taking place at Longbridge. By the end of 1969 the final Minis with Austin or Morris tags had rolled off the production line. Of these MkII Minis, 154,000 Austin and 206,000 Morris units were built.

As the sixties drew to a close, BMC was transformed into British Leyland, and the age of the MkIII Mini, the BL Mini, began. There was to be one basic 850 model, a

1000cc version, the newly introduced Clubman, (pitched as an up-market alternative), and the 1275GT, which was seen as the re-placement for the recently discontinued Mini Cooper. The front of the Mini was com-pletely redesigned for the Clubman and 1275GT (the word 'spoiled' is often pre-ferred by Mini devotees!) with a longer, squared-off front

*Inset, top: Two names, one car. Apart from their badges and grilles there was very little difference between the Austin ...
(Austin Seven De Luxe: 1962).*

*Inset, bottom: ... and the Morris, but BMC marketed them as different cars with separate images. (Morris Mini Minor: 1960).*

*The major Austin/Morris difference was the grille design. The Morris had vertical bars,
the Austin did not. (Morris Mini Minor: 1960).*

*The Innocenti Mini was a hit in Italy. Though, expensive, it was sophisticated, stylish and fun. This car sports the Mini Cooper grille badge unique to this model. (Innocenti Mini Cooper export: 1974).*

hydrolastic suspension was scuppered in favour of the original, tried and tested rubber cones, except on the Clubman and 1275GT (which were to revert two years later). Winding windows were introduced, and there were improvements to the electrics.

In 1975 the Clubman was fitted with the 1100cc engine, although the automatic version retained the 1000cc unit.

The 850 was replaced in mid-1979 by the City, which remained the base model, and the Super De Luxe (also an 850, but which shared the appointments of the 1000cc - which then became known as the Super!

The 850 versions were finally withdrawn in 1980, the City taking on the 1000cc engine. Over 400,000 of the 850 MkIII units had been built. The Clubman was discontinued sales of over 275,000 units. The Mini 1000 Super was discontinued in 1980 and replaced with the 1000HL, which borrowed heavily from both the Clubman and newly launched Metro. In 1982 it became the Mayfair, and went up-market, with better cloth seats, tinted glass and a radio. The City and Mayfair soldiered on until 1992, when the City was withdrawn and

*From 1980 the Mini received a larger, 34 litre (7.5 gallon) fuel tank - which helped keep the little wheels turning that bit longer. (Mini 1000 Automatic: 1980).*

and completely new grille and badge. The 1275GT was similar to the Clubman, except that it was fitted with a 1275cc engine, and front disc brakes from the Mini Cooper S. It sported a black front grille with red logo, and side-stripes proclaiming its name.

The Mini bodywork incorporated a number of changes for the better. Enclosed door hinges were a telling sign of modernisation, as were greatly improved panels and floorpan. The expensive

the Mayfair was re-launched with a 1300cc engine (courtesy of the Metro). Almost 1.5 million of the 1000cc versions were sold.

In 1992 the new basic Mini was christened the Sprite. It shared the 1300cc engine of the new Mayfair, the main difference between the two cars being the level of trim and equipment. The options are slightly different today, the Sprite has been replaced by the Rover Mini, with a Rover Cooper also available and a more up-market Rover Touring.

The Mini has always attracted attention - on its home ground and around the world. Japan proved a particularly lucrative market, and most European countries had their favourite Minis. France, for example, had special editions with the particularly English names of Twinings, After Eight and Woodbury, as well as the Printemps. while The Netherlands had the Ebony - black with stylish understated tartan seats.

At various times the Mini was manufactured abroad - in Australia, for example. There the Moke became a force to be reckoned with and Minis were produced from 1961 until 1977. There was a Mini K (for Kangaroo!), Mini SS, Mini Sunshine and Mini LS, as well as Cooper variants. Minis were also built by BMC's Spanish arm, AUTHI, in South Africa, and in South America, where several models of Mini with glass fibre bodies were made to comply with local regulations.

Perhaps the best known

*As Chile had no metal-pressing industry to call on, a fibreglass body shell was developed for Chilean Minis. (Chilean-built prototype 'Minicord': 1968).*

*Above & right, below: 50% extra - with a choice of two front ends or two back ends.*
*(Mini 850: 1971 and Mini Clubman: Wood & Pickett Margrave 1980).*

'foreign' Mini is the Italian Innocenti. The company had made its name first in metal pipework, and then as the maker of Lambretta Scooters. They first produced the Mini Minor 850 in 1965, followed the year after by their Mini Cooper version and an estate.

In 1974, with the company now under the BL umbrella,

the all-new Bertone-designed Mini 90 and 120 were introduced. Although based on the Mini, these cars were very different in appearance, with angular styling and a useful rear hatch. The BL/Innocenti connection was severed in 1975, and the company bought by De Tomaso, which continued making a car

based on the 120 until 1982. Innocenti Minis were also built in Belgium for export from 1973. The Belgian British Leyland plant was a prolific source of the Mini Special - a basic Mini body fitted with the 1100cc Clubman engine - from 1977 to 1981.

*Wood &
Pickett
interiors
were
always
lavish.
(Mini
Clubman
Margrave).*

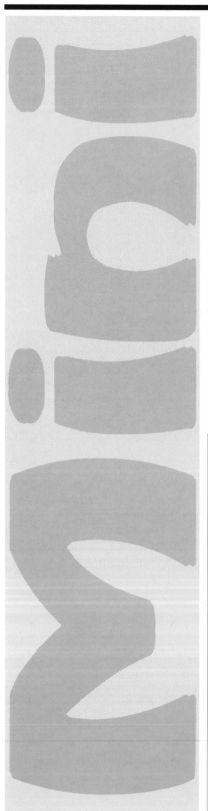

# WORK & PLEASURE

It was hardly surprising that the Mini would have commercial possibilities. Small, manoeuvrable, easily parked and individual, it was going to make an ideal small-load carrier. The Morris Minivan and the Austin Seven Van (to become the Austin Minivan two years later, in line with the saloons), made their debut at the beginning of 1960.

The vans were built on the Mini floorpan, the wheelbase

*The Austin Countryman and its counterpart the Morris Traveller were both available in 'woody' or all-metal versions. (Austin Mini Countryman: 1965).*

*The Countryman was pretty and practical, a compromise between saloon and van. (Austin Mini Countryman: 1965).*

*Estates and vans had hinged doors - primarily because they were cheaper to make. They allowed good access to the load space. (Minivan with rear windows: 1980).*

The van had seats for two, with a less-than-comfortable rear seat conversion available. (Minivan: 1980).

extended by four inches. The finished article, with overhang, was almost ten inches longer than the saloon. There was a huge rear load space (46cu ft to 58cu ft with the front passenger seat removed), and access through the twin back doors was easy thanks to the low load height. The interior appointment was spartan, with the absolute minimum of trim, and the front grille was of stamped metal for added economy.

Cost was one of the van's big plus points; having no rear windows it qualified as a commercial, and therefore attracted no purchase tax in the UK. From 1967, there was a 1000cc van on offer too. The van survived the British Leyland watershed, although, of course, the Austin and Morris names disappeared. Renamed simply the Mini Van, it continued in both 850cc and 1000cc guises until withdrawal in 1983. Total sales had reached over half a million.

The Pick-up was introduced at the start of 1961, and its life story ran in parallel with its Mini Van counterpart. Available in Morris Mini and Austin Seven (later Austin Mini) versions, then as the Mini Pick-up from 1969 until it was withdrawn in 1983, it sold almost 60,000 units in all.

The Pick-up was originally fitted with the 850cc engine; a 1000cc option became avail-

*Access to the pick-up's load area was via the drop-down tailgate. Because of the body shape, the rear lights were a unique fitting. (Mini Pick-up: 1976).*

able in 1967, although the smaller engine soldiered on until 1980. A canvas cover was offered for the load space - an optional extra at first, but later as standard.

The Estate versions of the Mini hit the road in September 1960, a year after their saloon counterparts. They were not designed specifically as commercials, but found

favour as dual-purpose vehicles - van in the week and car at the weekend. Traditional names from the two manufacturers were used - the Morris Mini Traveller and the Austin

Seven Countryman, which became the Austin Mini Countryman at the start of 1962, when the 'Seven' name was dropped from the saloon. They shared a floorpan with the Minivan, which had been introduced six months earlier.

The Traveller and Countryman 'woodies'- their wooden parts simply glued-on battens - came in one version only, with equipment based on the De Luxe saloon and with sliding windows at the rear. Double doors at the rear gave good access to the luggage space; with the rear seats folded down there was over 35 cu ft of space available, and when the seats were in use there was still more than 18 cu ft.

In 1962 an all-metal version of the cars was introduced to the UK market (it had been available for export for some eighteen months).

When the MkII Mini took over from the MkI in 1967, the Countryman and Traveller followed suit, both now fitted with the 1000cc engine; 'woody' and all-metal versions were available. Production of both Countryman and Traveller came to an end in 1969, after sales of 108,000 and 99,000, respectively.

With the start of the MkIII era, the Clubman estate took over. Although the wood of the 'woodies' had only been cosmetic, it was at least real.

Now the Clubman estate sported a swathe of imitation wood along its sides and across the rear doors. In 1977 this adornment gave way to painted stripes. Changes to the Clubman estate echoed those made to its saloon counterpart. However, it continued in production with the 1000cc engine for two years after the saloon's demise in 1980, badged as the 1000HL Estate. Just under 200,000 were made in all.

The first Mini Cabriolet appeared in June 1991. It was designed and built by the German Rover dealers LAMM, and Rover themselves were impressed enough to offer the car as a special edition of just

*This 1961 RAC van was in service in the West Midlands before being sold. It has been restored to RAC livery since it was discovered - painted bright pink! (Morris Minivan: 1961).*

*The Clubman Estate
started life with side
strips of fake wood -
saving trees after
taking over from the
'woody' perhaps? (Mini
Clubman Estate: 1978).*

seventy-five, to be sold
through selected Rover dealers in the UK. Mechanically the
Cabriolet was based on the
Cooper, with vital strengthen-
ing of the floorpan to com-
pensate for the lack of roof.
The body styling was very
butch, with huge tyres, flared
arches, side skirts, front spoiler
and integral bumpers. The
cars came in pearlescent red
paint, with the hood in ma-
roon. The interior was based
around the Mayfair, but with a
full-width woodgrain dash and
trimmings. The seventy-five
cars, although expensive,
were gone in a flash.

So successful and desir-
able were the LAMM cars that
Rover decided to put a
Cabriolet on the books as a
production model. It was
launched at the 1992
motorshow, and it differed
greatly from the LAMM version, which was still on sale in
Germany. It had been developed by Rover Special Products division in collaboration
with Karmann, and was built
by Rover themselves. Me-
chanically the Cabriolet was
based on the 1300 fuel-injected Cooper engine. The
cars came in two colours: blue
with grey hood or red with

*Both the Minivans and Mini Pick-ups retained their basic
interiors all the way through their production lives.
(Morris Minivan: 1968).*

red. The interior was luxuriously
appointed, with walnut dash
and trimmings, leather steering wheel and special cloth

and carpets. Such a desirable
car was also fitted with a full
alarm system and coded
stereo as standard.

*The good-looking Mini Cabriolet. It first appeared as a limited edition - not originally the idea of Rover, but of German Rover dealers LAMM. It joined the production models in 1993. (Mini Cabriolet: 1994).*

*Not everyone was prepared to wait thirty years for a Cabriolet! Crayford have been offering their stylish Mini Sprint and Mini Cooper Sprint conversions for many years. (Crayford Mini Cooper Sprint: 1962).*

*Alfresco lifestyle for the swinging sixties: this Crayford Cabriolet has the wine and the music.*

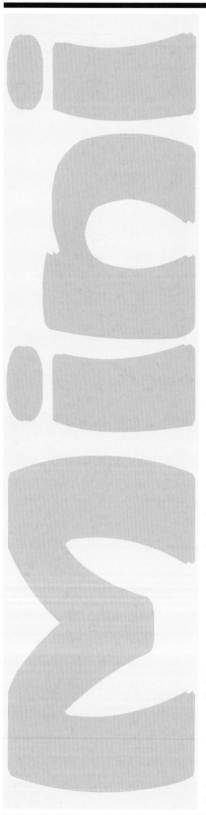

# SPECIAL EDITIONS

**4**

Special Editions have found their place in the marketing armoury of most small-car manufacturers. They are often produced in limited numbers - the limit sometimes only the number that the manufacturers can sell - and are often bright and cheerful affairs, invoking summer, sportiness, style, class or fun. As such they often come in for a deal of criticism from purists, but they bring a touch of relief from the rightly serious stuff of motoring - engineering, safety, economy and so on - and we should thank them for it. The Mini has flowered into more special editions than most: in the seventies two were produced; since 1983 there has been at least one (often more) announced each year. Mini milestones - 20, 25,30 and 35 years of production - have been celebrated with specials, as have the Monte Carlo successes and the car's film-star status.

The very first Mini Special Edition was produced in 1976. This was called the Limited Edition 1000, and 3,000 were built. It featured green and white paintwork with coachwork, extra chrome, and

brushed nylon seat covers in an orange stripe. The other seventies special was built to celebrate twenty years of the Mini in 1979. This was the 1100 Special, which became known simply as 1100S. It was fitted with the 1100cc engine from the Clubman, and with some of its more up-market interior fitments too. It could be purchased in either silver or metallic rose paintwork, and

*The special bonnet badge for the Mini 30. (Mini 30: 1989).*

featured wide alloy wheels, sports steering wheel and posh tartan seat covers. The intention was a run of 2500, but the 1100S production figures eventually reached over 5000.

The first of the eighties specials came along in 1983 - the Mini Sprite. Based on the City, but with some detail from the Mayfair, it had wide alloy wheels and came in a choice of red or yellow paint, with side stripes and a 'Sprite' logo above the rear wheel. Sales reached 2500 vehicles.

In 1984 the silver-painted Mini 25 came along, and 3500 were made. Based on the Mayfair, it sported 12-inch wheels, leather steering wheel, velvet trim, luxury carpets, and a stereo.

During the next three years there would be four special editions named after areas of London - in the City/Mayfair tradition. The Ritz made its appearance in 1985, with

*The Mini 30 was a real celebration, with a special paint finish in either pearlescent red (as here) or black, with a sumptuous interior. This car has been converted to Cooper status; the Cooper special edition of the following year was based on the 30 too. (Mini 30: 1989).*

The Mini was, of course, the real star of the film *The Italian Job*, in which Michael Caine and friends attempted a daringly audacious robbery with three Mini Coopers as get-away cars. (The Italian Job: 1992).

Left: Red Hot goes rallying. (Red Hot: 1988).

Special editions sold well abroad too - numbers from a limited production run would be set aside for particular export markets. This one is pictured in Italy. (Mini 30: 1989).

*Flame/Flame Red: 1989/90.*

*Racing/Racing Green: 1989/90.*

*Tahiti: 1993.*

*Neon: 1991.*

silver paint, alloy wheels and striped velvet trim. The following year the Chelsea arrived, again with alloys, and bright red paint. Although only 1500 were sold in the UK, many more were produced for export markets, and the Chelsea was a runaway success. Later the same year the Piccadilly followed, shining with gold paint and extra chrome, and with muted browns and reds for the interior. The Piccadilly sold particularly well in France, and production reached 2500.

The last of the 'Londoners' appeared in 1987. This was the Park Lane, which came in black, with classy velvet upholstery and a stereo. The Park Lane was as popular with export markets as the Chelsea had been, although 1500 were also sold in the UK.

The Park Lane was not the only Mini special of 1987. During the summer months, the Mini Advantage was introduced, sporting a tennis theme. The bodywork was white, with 'tennis net' decoration along the sides, a tennis ball motif on the Advantage logo, and green and grey seats and trim suggesting rackets and netting. Of over 4500 Advantages produced, more than half were sold in the UK.

A matching pair of Minis arrived for 1988. The exterior colours of Red Hot and Jet Black are self-explanatory; in addition both had black velour seats with red piping and signature-style logos on the seats as well as on their rear quarters and boot lids. The same year the Designer Mini appeared. This came in

either black or white, and was really a Mary Quant Mini, with the famous sixties designer's daisy motif on the bonnet badge and boss of the leather-bound steering wheel, and her signature on the black-and-white striped seats. 2000 were manufactured.

1989 was a bumper year for Mini special editions - five in all - although four were two sets of closely related twins, and one was a celebration! Racing and Flame came in British racing green and flame red respectively. They had white roofs and wheel trims and were fitted with a rev counter and sports steering wheel. Between the pair of them they reached sales of 2000. The second set of twins were Sky and Rose. While Racing and Flame were in primary colours, Sky and Rose were in pastels. They were white with light blue or pink roofs and colour-co-ordinated trim. Although charming, Sky and Rose were not to everyone's taste, and sales reached only 1000 in all.

Then came the Mini's thirtieth birthday, with great razzmatazz and the announcement of a special anniversary edition. The Mini 30 was available in two colours - black or pearlescent red. Both had smart coachwork and a special Mini crest bonnet badge which was repeated in decal form on the rear panels. These Minis had leather trim, stereo, alloy wheels and a brightwork front grille - they were very smart Minis indeed. Every Mini 30 owner - and there were 3000 of them in the UK alone - received a special Mini book in celebration of the car's achievements.

For 1990, the successful Racing Green and Flame Red special editions rode again, joined by a third, the Check Mate. The only really new features of the Racing and Flame cars this year were alloy wheels and engine modifications (courtesy of the Cooper). The Check Mate was the same, and came in black with a white roof. Between them the three sold well, and were popular export models - 2500 being sold in the UK alone. There was a Mini Cooper special this year, and yet another special, the Studio 2, which sold 2000 in the UK. The colour choice was black, blue or grey, with colour co-ordinated interior and a brightwork front grille.

In 1991 The Mini Neon appeared, with blue paintwork, chrome bumpers and velour trim, selling 1500 in all. This was also the year in which the Cabriolet was first introduced, as a very special special edition.

1992 was the year for the British Open Classic. This came with green paint, a wide, electrically operated canvas sunroof (for the 'open' feel), and tweed upholstery with leather inserts. The car, of which 1000 were sold in the UK, qualified to have Her Majesty the Queen's 'By Appointment' crest on the seats, too - not many cars can boast that. The same year saw the introduction of the none-too-serious Mini Italian Job, in honour of the 1969 film in which the cars starred. The Italian flag colours inspired a choice of red, white, blue or

green paint. The bonnet was decorated with faux strap stripes, the grille was given a retro feel with white paint, and alloy wheels were fitted. There was a special Italian Job badge too. Over 1700 were made, the majority sold in Britain.

In 1993 we had the Rio, a rare special because only 750 were made and it was sold only on the home market. It came in black, blue or turquoise, with a black and green interior. In the same year the Tahiti made its appearance - an even rarer sight than the Rio, with only 500 made. Tahiti was blue with alloy wheels, chrome bumpers and blue and black trim.

The big news for 1994 was, of course, another milestone - the Mini's 35th birthday. Launched in a blaze of publicity, the Mini 35 was resplendent in three colours: pearlescent red, metallic blue, or white. The 35 had an unusual blue and pink interior trim, alloys, and a brightwork grille. Sales totalled 1000 in all. The Cooper Special of 1994 celebrated the Monte Carlo successes. Then came the Mini Sidewalk in 1995, which was available in blue, grey or white with an attractive tartan trim and brightwork grille. A thousand of these were sold in all

In 1996 came a Cooper special anniversary edition, and the singular Equinox, with its unusual interior on a sun, moon and stars theme. Available in purple, grey or silver, with a chromed grille and matching decal, the Equinox seemed to suggest both the sixties and the nineties.

*British Open Classic: 1992.*

*Advantage: 1987.*

*Studio 2: 1990.*

*Chelsea: 1986.*

Twenty years of almost continuous Special Editions. Perhaps, by way of celebration, there should be a Special Edition!

*Jet Black: 1988.*

*Red Hot: 1988.*

*The Mini 25 was the first Mini special edition to be named after a birthday - and naturally came in silver in honour of the anniversary. (Mini 25: 1984)*

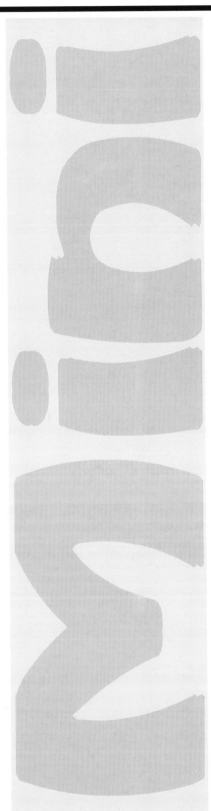

# 5
# ALL IN THE FAMILY

The workings of the corporate mind can be strange indeed. After just two years, the Mini was making a name for itself as the car of the moment. It seemed to appeal to customers not just for practical reasons, but also for its character and innovative design. So it is a little surprising to find BMC contriving not one but two 'up-market' models, and trying to mask their mini-ness with a dose of old-fashioned, British-style class. This thinking led to the Riley Elf and the Wolseley Hornet, Minis wearing the prestige badges of two of BMC's quality marques.

Of the two, the Riley was perceived to be slightly more up-market than the Wolseley. The Elf/Hornet design gave the Mini a boot section, a tradi-

*The poshest Mini, the Riley Elf, with the marque's traditionally shaped chrome grille, was created to sit on the top rung of the Mini ladder. (Riley Elf MkIII: 1967).*

*Inside the Riley all was wood, leather and good carpet, designed to appeal to the discerning British buyer. (Riley Elf MkIII: 1967)*

tional 'British' front grille, and the marks of a quality BMC interior: wood veneer, leather and comfortable seats. Outside there was much chrome embellishment, and the colour schemes were designed to whisper 'class' in a very discreet manner.

Both cars were fitted with the 850cc engine, but the extra body weight they had to carry made them less than nimble, and MkII versions were introduced at the start of 1963, driven by a 1000cc unit - which improved things enormously. From 1964 the cars were fitted with hydrolastic suspension. In 1966 the MkIII appeared, with winding windows and new-style interior door hinges - both improvements that would later find their way into the whole Mini range. There was an automatic option available from 1967, too.

The Riley Elf and Wolseley Hornet fill a rather curious corner of the Mini story, their peculiarities detracting from the Mini's essential style rather than adding to it; perhaps that was the idea. Nonetheless, they had a following: almost 31,000 Elfs and 29,000 Hornets were produced before the pair were withdrawn in 1969.

If the conception of the Elf and Hornet was strange, that of the Moke was odder still. Just as the Mini itself found its most successful niche was one for which it was never intended, so it was with the Moke. Its imagined destiny was to be a boring old utility workhorse that the armed services were expected to snap up in large quantities. But it was not to be. The prototype Moke suffered from ground-clearance problems, plus a lack of ability in the hill-climb-ing while load-carrying department. In other words, it wasn't up to the job, and no-one wanted to buy it.

Further prototypes with redesigned bodywork were built; still no-one wanted them. Next came the Twin-Moke, a four-wheel drive affair with two engines. This fared no better. So the decision was made to forget the services as a potential market, and to develop the Moke as a civilian workhorse instead.

The Moke was unveiled in 1964, as usual in both Austin and Morris versions, with the 850cc standard Mini engine. The response was frankly underwhelming. Although cheap, qualifying as a com-

*The Riley's 'booted Mini' rear view. Most Elf and Hornet models came in a two-tone paint scheme (Riley Elf MkIII: 1967).*

*If the Elf was destined for the top, the Hornet's place was just below. The Wolseley Hornet carried the marque's traditional lit badge on the radiator. (Wolseley Hornet MkII: 1964).*

mercial vehicle and therefore escaping purchase tax, the Moke was highly unsuitable for the British climate, and although it enjoyed a brief Slone-type popularity, it was never a sixties hit.

The writing was on the wall when in 1967 the Moke was reclassified as a proper car and the added tax immediately increased the price.

BMC called a halt in 1968 and withdrew the Moke. Less than 15,000 had been built, with only around 1500 sold in the UK.

The Moke was down but not out. It had been in production in Australia for two years in BMC's manufacturing plant in Sydney, where it was fitted with the more suitable 1000cc engine, and known as

the Morris Mini Moke. It sold well, suited to the more favourable Australian weather conditions. In 1969 a MkII version was issued. By now it was called the BMC Mini Moke and was fitted with a larger 1000cc engine, and larger 13-inch wheels, as well as upgraded brakes and drive and better cooling. The all-important Mini word was

*The Hornet's interior was marginally less superior than that of the Elf, with a three-instrument centre panel rather than a full-width dash. (Wolseley Hornet MkII: 1964).*

*Left: Although so similar, the Elf and Hornet were given separate images and sold through different outlets - just as the Morris and Austin Minis had been. (Wolseley Hornet MkII: 1964).*

dropped in 1970 in favour of the BMC Moke, although the name changed again two years later, becoming the Leyland Moke.

Meanwhile, a special edition had been launched - the Californian - which was fitted with a 1300cc engine plus a fair number of extras. It lasted only two years, but was re-launched in 1977, when like all other Mokes it was fitted with the 1000cc engine. A

pick-up version was available from 1974. Minor improvements were made to the Moke in 1979, including a new hood that could be closed with zippers. Moke production ceased in Australia in 1981, after more than 26,000 units had been sold.

Still the Moke wouldn't lie down. Assembly had been going on in Portugal, using parts imported from Australia, since 1980. The Moke under-

This Moke was bought as a wreck and lovingly restored in fun colours that suit it admirably. Unfortunately for BMC, they did not pitch the Moke as a fun buggy - it found that niche later. (rebuilt Moke: 1964).

Bouquets to the Australians for seeing the Moke's possibilities - they made it famous! (Rebuilt Moke: 1964).

*Left: Mokes originally came with the minimum of fittings and fixtures. Although this one is updated and up-rated, the functional feel remains. (rebuilt Moke: 1964).*

went a few changes to rationalise its production and keep down costs, including the introduction of 12-inch wheels. It gained in popularity - not so much as a utility vehicle as originally intended, but as a stylish fun car that was practical too.

In celebration of the quarter-century of the Moke, a Moke 25 with relevant badging was introduced, but

shortly afterwards Rover stopped production in Portugal, with total production numbering less than 10,000 units. At various times these Portuguese Mokes were imported into Britain - coming full circle indeed! Finally, the rights to the Moke were sold to the Italian firm Cagiva, and production began again. The Moke story continues.

*The Moke was planned as a military vehicle, but gradients and ground clearance were a problem. (British Transport Police Moke: 1965).*

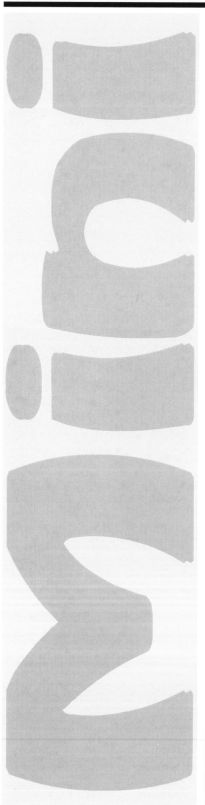

# STRANGE MINIS

## 6

The Mini Marcos was officially launched at the Earls Court Racing Car Show early in 1966. Later that year, a Marcos BMC - supported by the BMC Competitions Department - was entered at Le Mans. The little car finished in a highly respectable 15th place, the only British car to finish that year. The Marcos was success-ful not only on the track: four of its land speed class records survive to this day, and the cars regularly notch up wins in group K (kitcar) races, historic sports races, sprints and hillclimbs.

In addition to the cars produced by Marcos at their works in Bradford-on-Avon, some have been made under licence in Ireland and South Africa.

*Stretching the point. Lindsay Haynes spent more than 4000 hours over eighteen months converting two standard Minis into this classy 14-foot limousine.*

*Penny Lane: homage to the Beatles song from another star of the sixties, the Mini. This one is covered completely in British pre-decimal pennies.*

The Outspan driveable Orange is a very strange Mini. A prototype of the promotional vehicle was first tested in 1972. It had a hinged top half, but the opening mechanism made it far too heavy to be practical. The door was relocated at the back and six of the cars were made. Five were used extensively in promotional campaigns in the UK, France and Germany, and one was destined for South

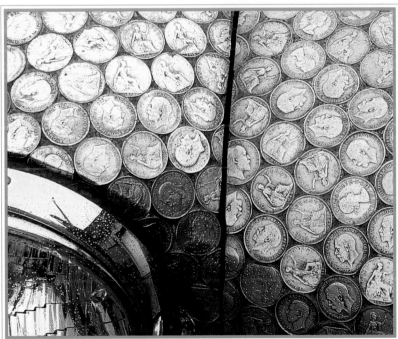

Built by Andy Saunders, 'Claustrophobia' was featured in the 1988 Guinness Book of Records as the lowest car in the world.

'Claustrophobia' started life as a Mini. The car has been reduced in height by 14 inches, with the result that the windscreen is only six inches high. The engine protrudes through the bonnet, and getting in is ... tricky.

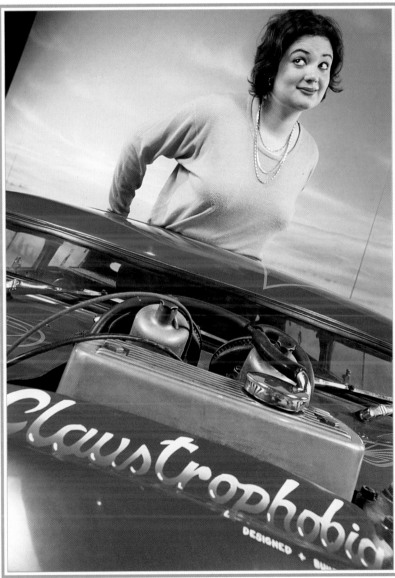

*Based on a 1963 Mini, this car has been rebuilt and reshaped by Scott Lloyd. The car is nine inches lower than standard, and the revision gives a futuristic Japanese concept-car look from the rear.*

*The Orange's interior is overwhelmingly ... orange. Colour co-ordination taken to its limits. The tinted windows turn the world outside orange too.*

The Capespan driveable Orange - just what a girl needs to time-travel through the centuries - the Orange, Tardis-style.

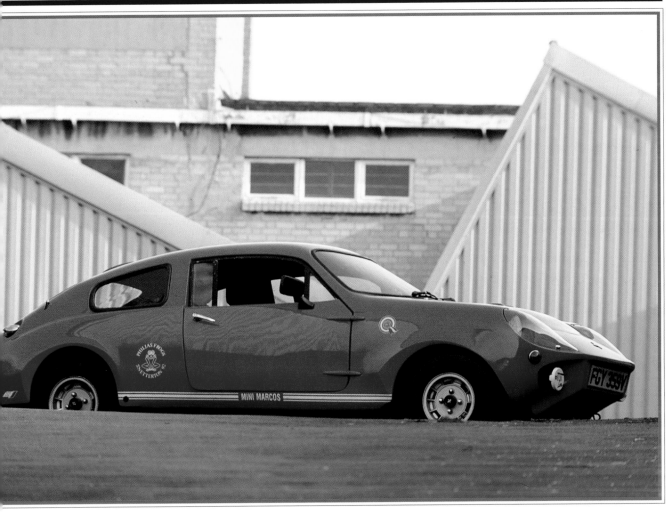

*Mini Marcos MkIV based on 1971 Mini Cooper S: 1979.*

Africa. Of the five European Oranges, one was scrapped in 1981, while another was renovated in 1980 and appeared in the Mini's 21st birthday exhibition, after which it was donated to the National Motor Museum at Beaulieu, where it is still on show.

The remaining Oranges have taken part in fetes, shows and processions all over Europe. They were re-fitted and re-sprayed in 1993 and are now enjoying a new lease of life. The Oranges have a short, tubular space frame chassis which gives a 48-inch wheelbase. A front subframe supports the 1000cc engine, automatic gearbox and suspension. The rear supports the rear suspension and the 200lb of ballast required to keep the Orange stable. Driving the Orange is an acquired skill, as the pedals are situated at the bottom of a narrow shaft which takes the driver's right leg only! Ventilation is nil. The inside of the car is covered all round - literally - in orange-dyed fabric, and the view from the orange-tinted side windows (mercifully not the windscreen!) is downright weird. But how could the Orange be anything but fun to drive and to watch, topped off by its cheeky green 'stalk'.

*Left: Orange a la Duck.*

*Overleaf: Mini Jem MkII based on 1971 Mini.*

*Mini Marcos MkV based on 1977 Mini: 1993.*

*90s-style Coupe Mini built by UK-based Church Green under licence from Broadspeed.*

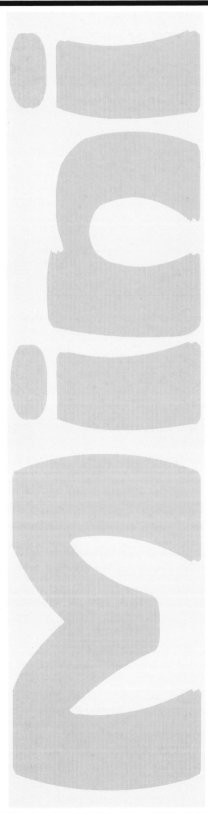

# THE COOPER STORY

**7**

If Alec Issigonis had prevailed at the outset, the world-famous Mini Cooper might never have gone into production. No matter that John Cooper, already a successful and respected racing car builder, was interested in his product; Issigonis felt that the Mini had been conceived as a family saloon car, not as a sports racer, and he would have preferred it to stay that way. Fortunately, Cooper persuaded BMC managing director Sir George Harriman that his idea was a good one, and BMC duly built the thousand cars required to qualify the Mini for Group 2 racing. In 1961 the Mini Cooper was launched as a production

*Thirty years after his victory in the 1964 Monte Carlo Rally, Paddy Hopkirk returned to take part again in 1994. This limited edition was brought out to celebrate. (Mini Cooper Monte Carlo: 1994).*

*John Parnell's beautiful 970cc Cooper S - one of a very rare breed. (Austin Cooper S: 1964).*

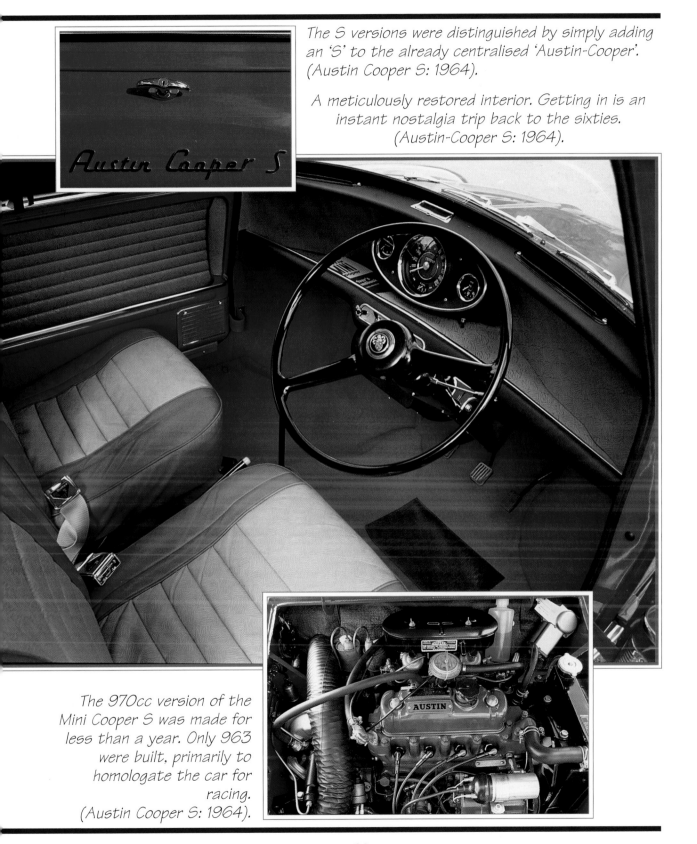

The S versions were distinguished by simply adding an 'S' to the already centralised 'Austin-Cooper'. (Austin Cooper S: 1964).

A meticulously restored interior. Getting in is an instant nostalgia trip back to the sixties. (Austin-Cooper S: 1964).

*Austin Cooper S*

The 970cc version of the Mini Cooper S was made for less than a year. Only 963 were built, primarily to homologate the car for racing. (Austin Cooper S: 1964).

Left: The dapper Monte Carlo is always well turned out. (Mini Cooper Monte Carlo: 1994).

Right: The special edition Mini Cooper 35 was brought out in 1996 to celebrate the anniversary of the first Coopers.

The Monte Carlo winners certainly set the rally alight. (Road version of 1994 Monte Carlo Rally car).

Swedish drivers Lars Fritz and Ulf Lindberg putting their Mini Cooper through its paces at the Old-timer Grand Prix meeting at the Nurburgring. (Morris Mini Cooper S: 1964).

Inset: The 'Mighty Minis' racing events were devised by Roger Tello as a series for everyone who enjoys racing, even if they operate on a tight budget. The cars race on the top circuits, and the action is fast and furious. (Paul Clark's 'Mighty Mini').

by the press and by potential customers; by the time the Cooper had been on the market for a year it represented one in five of all Mini sales. Works teams were entered for the major rallies and soon started turning in impressive results, culminating in the famous Monte Carlo Rally wins of 1964, 1965 and 1967. (Minis stormed home ahead in 1966 too, but they were disqualified, along with other British competitors, on a very suspect technicality of lighting specification).

Like the other Minis the first Coopers came in both Austin Seven Cooper (later Austin Mini Cooper) and Morris Mini Cooper forms. Fitted with 1000cc engines - actually the 997cc unit - they were the first Minis ever to sport a unit any larger than the 850cc. Visually the Coopers were distinctive because of their contrasting roof colour, while inside they were well appointed, in line with their top-of-the-range image.

From 1964, the Coopers received the engine from the Elf and Hornet (998cc) but with better performance than before, and also hydrolastic suspension. The previous year, however, a new Mini Cooper model had been introduced - the Mini Cooper S - in both Austin and Morris guises. This was fitted with the 1071cc engine, and was externally the same as before. In 1964 a 970cc engined version arrived. It was expensive to make, and although popular with the racing fraternity it was in production for only a few months and not many were made. In this year, too, the

Cooper S 1275cc was introduced. This became available in single-colour options as well as the familiar Cooper two-tone, and it was upgraded in 1966 with twin fuel tanks and a better suspension system.

In parallel with the MkII Mini in 1967 came the Mini Cooper MkII and Mini Cooper S MkII, incorporating all the production changes of ordinary production Minis. The standard Mini Cooper was withdrawn in 1969, but the Mini Cooper S soldiered on. A MkIII version was introduced in 1970, taking much of its trim from the newly introduced Clubman. Then with the seventies came the British Leyland era and a new style of management - one which believed most strongly in rationalisation and paring down costs to a minimum. The Mini Cooper was just able to celebrate ten years of production, and then its part of the story was over. In all, over 100,000 Mini Coopers had been made, a quarter of them of the S variety. John Cooper, of course, did not disappear from view! Actively engaged in all aspects of the motor industry, including motorsport, he continued to produce Mini Coopers at his own facility, as conversions from production models.

Things often come full circle, and Rover would prove a different animal from both BMC and British Leyland. In 1989 Rover offered the John Cooper performance conversion kits for the 1000cc Mini through their dealerships. The following year Rover Special Products designed a very special edition indeed: a

model - with the blessing of Issigonis, who had eventually been persuaded by the obvious potential of the idea.

The new Mini was greeted with amazement and delight,

*Mini Cooper in British racing green - a classic example of the most famous and popular British car ever. (Mini Cooper: 1991).*

limited run of 1650 Mini Coopers (1000 for the UK), fitted with a 1275cc engine. The colour choice was British racing green, red or black, all with white roofs and white bonnet stripes and with John Cooper's signature in pride of place. Extra special fittings included a red leather steering wheel, red carpets and spotlamps. Needless to say, these special cars were quickly snapped up and remain highly sought-after to this day.

Within a few months the new Mini Cooper had joined the ranks as a regular production model (signed body stripes, driving lamps and sunroof were optional extras).

Then in 1991 came another performance kit, this time creating a Mini Cooper S. Later that year the Mini Cooper got a fuel-injected, catalized version of the 1275cc engine to comply with emission controls, and it became known as the Mini Cooper 1.3i. A revised 'S' conversion kit soon followed, which produced the Mini-Cooper Si.

In 1994 the Mini Cooper was treated to a special edition. The Mini Cooper Monte Carlo began life as an add-on kit, available when the car was bought new, at no extra cost, and comprising extra driving lamps plus a host of decals, including the John Cooper signature, Monte

Carlo Rally stickers and racing-type door panels. The kit was offered as part of a promotion to celebrate the 30th anniversary of Paddy Hopkirk's 1964 Rally win. Hopkirk revisited past glories by taking part in the 1994 rally, and a Mini Cooper Monte Carlo special edition was produced in celebration. This was a 200-car limited edition, available in black or red, with a luxurious retro red and cream interior. Gun-metal alloy wheels, wide tyres, extra spot-lamps and decals in the Monte Carlo style completed the picture. In addition thirty-five Grand Prix specials were built, with 86bhp engines.

The Mini Cooper 35

*Both pages: Not the new Mini, but a taste of things to come? The ACV30 shows us the type of car that Rover might have chosen to race in 1997. Would it have been a winner? (Rover Mini Cooper S ACV30: 1997).*

emerged in 1996, a 200-car special celebrating 35 years of the Mini Cooper. It was painted almond green - the same colour as the very first Cooper of 1961 - and was fitted with gun-metal alloys and two extra spot-lamps, plus green leather seats and trim. The Mini range today includes the Rover Cooper, with an optional S-pack.

The 1997 Monte Carlo Rally had a few surprises in store. The thirtieth anniversary of the completion of the 1964/65/67 hat trick of wins in the Rally saw laps of honour by the three winners - Paddy Hopkirk, Timo Makinen and Rauno

Aaltonen. With them drove a strangely familiar yet altogether new motor car - the Rover Mini Cooper ACV30. This Anniversary Concept Vehicle in celebration of that thirty-year milestone will not be a production car. Jointly developed by Rover and partners

BMW, it claims only to represent the Mini as it might have been entered in 1997 as a rally super-car. It is a stunning sight in bright red, with that evocative white roof and bonnet stripes. It has Mini proportions, although its lines are more sculptured and rounded.

The ACV30 is not the Mini of the future, but it certainly portrays the spirit of the Mini in futuristic form. The Mini's replacement is expected around the millennium and Rover are adamant that, whatever else, the new Mini will be fun - so no change there!

Gallery

*Crayford Mini Cooper Sprint: 1962*

Wood and Pickett Margrave-style Mini: 1966.

Morris Mini MkII: 1969.

Austin-Cooper S: 1964.

Mini Cooper Monte Carlo (1994) & Mini Cooper (1991).

Dear Reader,
We hope you have enjoyed this Veloce Publishing production. If you have ideas for other automotive books, please write and tell us. Meantime, Happy Motoring!

There are also Veloce Colour Family Albums on Bubblecars & Microcars (two), Vespa, Lambretta, VW Beetle, Citroen DS, Citroen 2CV and VW Bus. More titles are in preparation.

# Photographer's postscript

The photographs in this book were all taken with Leica R6 cameras and Leica lenses ranging from 16mm fisheye to 560mm. Film used was Fujichrome - mostly Velvia, with the occasional roll of Provia. The photographic sessions were varied, and covered a period of just over a year.

I must thank especially Trevor Morgan and Don Shaw of Capespan for the session involving the Mini Oranges, and also Pauline Chart for a superb rendition of a frozen Nell Gwynn. In the town of Buckingham, the Mystic Mini

Club really pulled out all the stops, with Tony Miles and Tracy Peacock (helped by Sue Birch and Lance Peacock) doing a thoroughly convincing time-warp back to the sixties.

On a January morning I travelled to Oxford to see Mike Scarfe's fibreglass Mini. The previous day had started with fog, burning off to a brilliant sunny day, and the same was forecast for this day. Except, instead of burning off, the fog got thicker and thicker. Mike drove me into the city centre, where we continued the photography in

that eerie silence that heavy fog brings. Later in the afternoon I met up with Stephen Smith and Tracy Napier and, still in dense fog (freezing, by now), we watched the light disappear at Newbury Fire Station.

Throughout this project, we have had the contined support of Roger 'the Hat' Wall, one of the Mini's strongest supporters. His knowledge and enthusiasm have been extraordinary, and it is only fitting that he should appear (on page 92) with his car - and wearing one of his hats!

David Sparrow

96